A Long, Long Road Back To Love

A Lenten Congregational Resource with Sermons, Skits and Children' Sermons

Arley K. Fadness

CSS Publishing Company, Inc.
Lima, Ohio

A LONG, LONG ROAD BACK TO LOVE

FIRST EDITION
Copyright © 2019
by CSS Publishing Co., Inc.

Library of Congress Cataloging-in-Publication Data -

Names: Fadness, Arley K., 1937- author.
Title: A long, long road back to love : prodigal kids and a loving father /
  Arley K. Fadness.
Description: FIRST EDITION. | Lima, Ohio : CSS Publishing Company, Inc.,
  2019. | Includes bibliographical references and index.
Identifiers: LCCN 2018059110 (print) | LCCN 2019011374 (ebook) | ISBN
  9780788029431 (eBook) | ISBN 0788029436 (eBook) | ISBN 9780788029424 (pbk.
  : alk. paper) | ISBN 0788029428 (pbk. : alk. paper)
Subjects: LCSH: Prodigal son (Parable)--Miscellanea. | Bible. Luke, XV,
  11-32--Criticism, interpretation, etc.
Classification: LCC BT378.P8 (ebook) | LCC BT378.P8 F33 2019 (print) | DDC
  226.8/06--dc23

For more information about CSS Publishing Company resources, visit our website at www.csspub.com, email us at csr@csspub.com, or call (800) 241-4056.

e-book:
ISBN-13: 978-0-7880-2943-1
ISBN-10: 0-7880-2943-6

ISBN-13: 978-0-7880-2942-4
ISBN-10: 0-7880-2942-8

Contents

An Introduction

Garrison Keillor, former host of the *Prairie Home Companion* radio show, was asked in an interview about all the honors he had received or turned down. He said, "Last year (2001), I was inducted into the American Academy of Arts and Letters, and that's all the honor I need until I die. And afterward – no eulogy at my funeral. Just tell the story of the prodigal son, sing "Amazing Grace" and let it go at that."

"Christians have perverted the message of Christ," says the Muslim to his Christian friend. "The story of the prodigal son proves that the cross is unnecessary for forgiveness. The boy comes home. His father welcomes him. There is no cross and no incarnation. Islam, with no cross or Savior preserves the true message of Christ."
(*The Cross and the Prodigal* by Kenneth Bailey, p. 9)

This Middle East centuries-old criticism begs an answer and spurs Christians to revisit one of Jesus' greatest and well-loved parables.

The context for the parable of the prodigal son in Luke 15 finds Jesus in conflict with the Pharisees. Jesus is seen talking to and teaching the tax collectors and "sinners."
The Pharisees murmur, "this man welcomes sinners and eats with them."
Hearing the Pharisee's criticism, Jesus tells three stories to rebuke the murmuring, muttering Pharisees.

The progression of the three stories in Luke 15, a lost sheep, a lost coin, and a lost son, moves from the larger to the lesser in numbers.

Story one sees the lost sheep found as one in one hundred. Story two tells about the one lost coin in ten that is found. In story three, the lost is about one in two sons that is found.
In all three stories, when the lost is found there is an explosion of joy and celebration!

Theme Song

"A Song of Jesus"

Text: Arley K. Fadness
Music: Ed Johnson

1. A father old, he had two sons, his love for them was strong,
As sons grew up he trusted that they never would do wrong.
Upon a ranch they played and worked, fed goats and camels too,
Friends for life, both sons and dad, bonded, it seemed good and true.

2. But then one day the younger son said, "Dad, can't stay no more,"
My dreams, my hopes, my longing eyes a distant land adore.
I want my third, I want my due, I want, I want right now.
It pained the father's heart, yet sadly now he must allow.

Chorus: Kyr-i-e, kyr-i-e e-le-i-son. Beloved sons you'll always be!

3. In a distant land the son kicked back and sowed his wild oats,
He spent his "dough" then famine struck – he knew he'd soon be toast."
Down on his luck, he got a job, a feeding hogs and swine,
Foolish lad, hungry lad, eating corn, alas, no more wine.

4. Then one day his dark mind awoke, his heart grew bright with hope.
I must go back to my dad's house for here I cannot cope.
His bag packed up, he left the sty, and running homeward bound
He wondered if his dad would let him be a slave who plows the ground.

Chorus: Kyr-i-e kyr-i-e e-le-i-son, Beloved sons you'll always be!

5. The loving dad, eye to the east, saw his son coming fast,
His heart leaped up, tears filled his eyes, "My son, my son, at last!"
A sprint, a hug, a warm embrace, a shout of joy he gave,
"A robe, a ring, a fatted calf, for this is my son, not my slave!"

6. Come to the dance, be merry, eat, the lost is fin'ly found,
Forgiveness, grace, and mercy too abundantly abound.
Not judging nor condemning be -- as was the elder son.
For God's love will find us anywhere that we may run.

Chorus: Kyr-i-e, Kyr-i-e e-le-i-son.
Beloved ones we'll always be!
Beloved ones we'll always be!

Note to Keyboard Accompanist

For convenience and enhancement of the flow put piano accompaniment
page 1 opposite page 2. Then put page 3 opposite page 4.

This arrangement makes it much easier in which there is only
one page turned instead of five times.

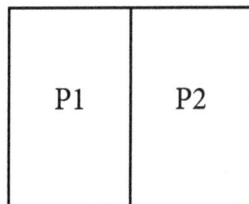

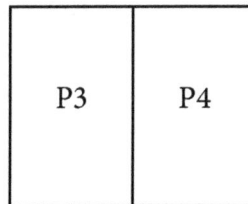

P1	P2

P3	P4

A Song of Jesus

verses 1 and 2

Arley Fadness
Ed Johnson

A
fath - er old he had two sons his love for them was strong. As
then one day the young - er son said Dad can't stay no more, My

sons grew up he trust - ed that they nev - er would go wrong Up -
dreams, my hopes, my long - ing eyes a dis - tant land a - dore. I

on the ranch they played and worked, fed goats and cam - els too,
want my third, I want my due, I want, I want right now. It

Friends for life, both sons and dad, bond - ed, it seemed good and
pained the fath - er's heart yet sad - ly now he must al -

true But low. Kyr - i - e, kyr - i - e

e - le - i - son. Be - lov - ed sons you'll al - ways be!

A Song of Jesus
verses 3 and 4

Arley Fadness
Ed Johnson

In a dis - tant land the son kicked back and sowed his wild oats. He
one day his dark mind a - woke, his heart grew bright with hope. I

spent his dough then fam - ine struck he knew he'd soon be toast Down
must go back to my dad's house for here I can not cope. His

on his luck he got a job a feed - ing hogs and swine
bag packed up, he left the sty, and run - ning home - ward bound He

Fool - ish lad, hun - gry lad, eat - ing corn a - las no more
won - dered if his dad would let him be a slave who plows the

wine. Then
ground.

Kyr - i - e, kyr - i - e e - le - i - son.

Be - lov - ed sons you'll al - ways be.

A Song Of Jesus

verses 5 and 6

Arley Fadness
Ed Johnson

The lov - ing dad, eye to the east, saw his son com - ing fast, His
to the dance, be mer - ry, eat; the lost is fin - 'ly found For -

heart leaped up, tears filled his eyes, "my son, my son, at last!" A
give - ness, grace and mer - cy too a - bun - dant - ly a - bound. Not

sprint, a hug, a warm em - brace, a shout of joy he gave A robe, a ring, a fat - ted calf
jud - ging nor con - demn - ing be as was the eld - er son. For God's love will find us

"For this is my son, not my slave." Come
an - y where that we may run.

Kry - i - e, kry - i - e e - le - i - son.

Be - lov - ed ONES WE'LL al - ways be, Belov - ed ONES WE'LL al - ways be!

11

A Song of Jesus

piano accompaniment

Arley Fadnes
Ed Johnson

♩=85

Introduction

VERSES

The notation indicates that the enclosed note should only be played in verse 3

ending for vs 1 & 3
verses 2 & 4 to chorus
r.h.
CHORUS
ENDING FOR FIRST CHORUS (after vs 2)
return for VERSE 3 (at measure 3)
r.h.
ENDING FOR SECOND CHORUS (after vs 4)

23
VERSES 5 & 6
26
28
5
5
30
ENDING for VERSE 5
(return to measure 23 for verse 6)
5
r.h.

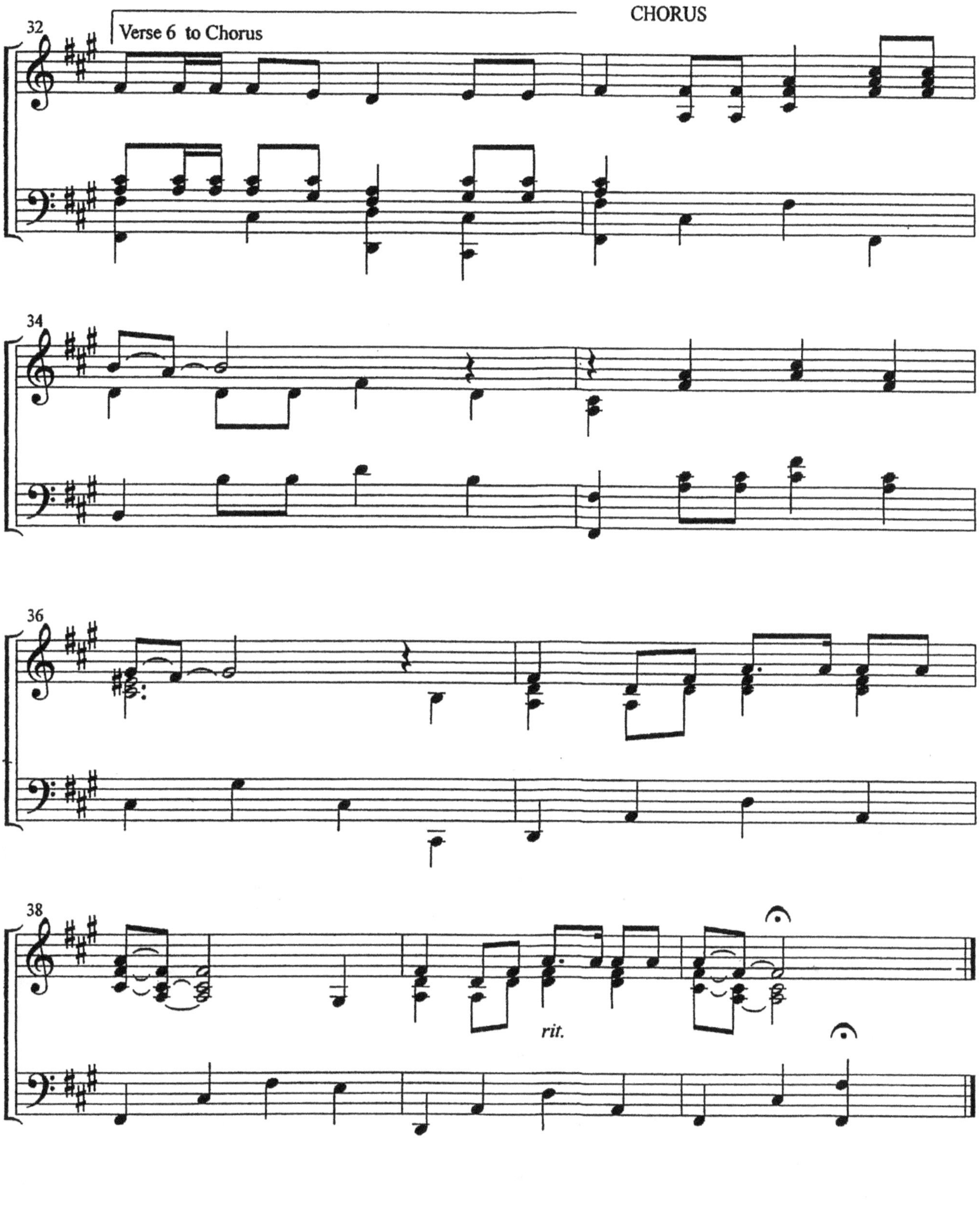
32
Verse 6 to Chorus
CHORUS
34
36
38
rit.

Week One

"DAD, I'M DREAMING"

Talking Hats
(Children's Mission Minute)

Props: Hats, Caps, and various Lids
Setting: Imagining a hat that talks – and oh, the story it tells

Mission Minute One

Hello Boys and Girls,

What kind of a hat am I wearing? (Wears cowboy/cowgirl hat)
You're right, it's a cowboy hat.
Notice my cowboy hat has a brim that tilts upward like a smiley face. It is a happy hat.
It's happy because it gives shade from the hot sun. It's happy because it protects from dusty wind and cold rain. It's happy because it can even be used as a bucket for oats to
feed and water your horse.
Oh my, if my hat could talk, it could tell you lots of things.

So let's pretend my hat *can* talk.

(Takes hat off and uses as a puppet)

Mr. (Ms.) Hat, we can see you are smiling with your brim turned up. We would like to ask you just "why are you so happy?"

(Hat starts talking)

Happy Hat: *"Well boys and girls, I am a happy hat because the cowboy or cowgirl who wears me, loves God and knows that God loves all people – rich, poor, tall, short, black, and white. All are precious in God's sight. I am smiling knowing God's love shines down on me, and I, in turn, get to love other people too."*

Like who Happy Hat?

Happy Hat: *"Well, especially those moms and dads and kids who are poor and hungry. Some are weak and sick. Some have clothes that are tattered and torn or none at all. Who you ask? Just open your eyes. Of course, poor people who want a better life.*

How do you do that?

Happy Hat: *"Have you ever heard of 'passing the hat?'"*

Oh, Yes we all have heard of "passing the hat."

Happy Hat: *"Just turn me upside down like this and pass me around. People who are good-hearted, blessed and generous put money and love into me. And I in turn, am able to give animals like heifers, goats, pigs, water buffalo, chickens, geese, and rabbits to poor people who can then earn a living and have a better life."*

Wow Happy Hat! That is amazing and that makes me happy too. Is this gifting through Heifer Project International?

Happy Hat: *"Yes, yes it is and then you know what? These poor people pass a Happy Hat again amongst themselves and give the first baby animal to another poor family.*
It's the gift that keeps on giving.

I am impressed Happy Hat. Thanks for sharing.

Let us pray:
Lord Jesus by your love on the cross you have shown us the way of love.
You have given us so much – food, clothing, shelter, pets, school, and church.
Give to us one more thing and that is a grateful and generous heart.
Amen

A Restless Lad
(A chancel drama)

Setting: Counselor's office
Characters: Dr. Fad
              A Lad – Chad

Lad knocks timidly.

Fad: C'mon in. I'm Dr. Fad. Thanks for making this appointment and coming in. I see your name is Chad.

Lad: Yeah. Oh hi. I, I, aah decided to come in for a little talk with you Dr. Fad.

Fad: Great. Have a seat. Sooooo.....

Lad: I've been meaning to talk to you about well – ah, ahem, you know about this *friend*. He's got this problem.

Fad: Your *friend* has a problem?

Lad: Yeah, I sort of, I think so.

Fad: Are you at liberty to tell me about it?

Lad: Sure.

Fad: Well?

Lad: Aah....

Fad: Go ahead – everything's confidential here.

Lad: All right. Well you see this *friend* is really bored.

Fad: Bored? Like disinterested in what's going on?

Lad: Yeah, bored blue.

Fad: So what is he bored about?

Lad: Bored with school.

Fad: Is he smart?

Lad: I guess.

Fad: Anything at school that is particularly boring?

Lad: Most everything – aah – he says.

Fad: Is he bored anywhere else?

Lad: Bored at church too.

Fad: Church? You mean like at worship?

Lad: Yeah, Dr. Fad, same ole, same ole.

Fad: Sermon boring?

Lad: Oh yeah!

Fad: Liturgy?

Lad: Of course.

Fad: I agree Chad, a lot of things we participate in when they become routine tend to seem boring especially to a young person like yourself – ah, er, I mean your *friend*.

Lad: Yeah, he's really restless. Fidgety. Always watching travel videos like the Rick Steves' stuff you know.

Fad: Restless? Travel videos? Rick Steves? Hmmm. Anything else?

Lad: Yeah, he's tired of his folks.

Fad: Are his folks abusive? Neglectful? Controlling? Does he have bad parents?

Lad: Nah, none of that. He's got great parents. He's just tired of 'em.

Fad: Tired of his parents?

Lad: Well yeah. He loves 'em and stuff but just dissatisfied with their old fashioned ways I guess. He'd like to go to Alaska.

Fad: Alaska?

Lad: Work in the fisheries. On a boat *(excitedly)* out in the deep blue....or go to Hawaii.

Fad: And do what in Hawaii?

Lad: Be a beach bum. *(laughs)*

Fad: You know Chad, you seem to know your *friend* pretty well. I wonder if he isn't looking for something.

Lad: Like what Dr. Fad?

Fad: Like ah perhaps fulfillment. A purpose in life. Something that gives him meaning.

Lad: Oh yeah, oh awesome yeah! You got it Dr. Fad.

Fad: We need to end our session today but let's talk some more at the next session – and ah by the way could you bring your *friend* along?

Lad: Aah, aah, can't you and I just talk between the two of us?

Fad: Sure – whatever suits you. Thanks for coming in Chad. Bye.

Lad: Bye and thank you Dr. Fad.

Lad leaves. Counselor says to herself (himself), "He thinks we're talking about his friend." *(Turns to the audience and winks) I know better who he's talking about –*
and you know who too!"

Dreamer
(A Message)

Luke 15: 11 "There was a man who had two sons. The younger of them said to his father, 'father give me the share of the property that belongs to me.'"

"Oh no," I groaned as I stepped out of my apartment that Monday morning in North Minneapolis. I was on my way to work. I looked curbside. No car. My just-paid-for 1955 black classic hardtop Chevy was gone! Towed? Stolen? Lost? As a seminary student I could hardly afford to lose my car, my transportation to work. I knew it was a rough neighborhood that I lived in that summer – but was it that rough?

I reported the stolen car to the police and caught a bus to work to downtown St. Paul. I was bummed all day. That evening my roommate Gary invited me to go with him to visit his relatives in south Minneapolis. On the way – guess what? I glanced down a certain alley, miles and miles away from the apartment and there was my beloved black '55 Chevy.

I found my own car! Police wouldn't believe it. They eyed me suspiciously.
You just don't find your own stolen car in a city like Minneapolis/St. Paul.
But I did. I found it. Miracle or what?

Same thing happened in the greatest parable Jesus ever told! Something lost is found.
Something far more valuable than a '55 Chevy. A *lost son* comes home. He is found!

The power of the parable of the prodigal son is seeing one's self in the story! You and I at one time or another in our lives are there in the lives of the younger son or the elder brother. That's us. And by God's grace we hear the Father calling us home.

The Pharisees decided to pick a fight with Jesus. They caught Jesus eating with tax collectors and "sinners." They muttered, "this man welcomes sinners and eats with them."
Jesus responded by telling three unforgettable parables recorded in Luke 15.

A lost sheep is found. A lost coin is found. A lost son comes home. The progression moves from the many to the one. One lost sheep in a hundred is found. One lost coin in ten is found. One lost son of two is found. And in all three parables, when the lost is found there's joy, joy, joy.

You know the story. The son left home one day in eager search for something better, only to return home another day and find there what he was really seeking. In his father's house he discovered what he had so vainly sought in a distant country – right there in the place from which he had run away.

What brought the wayward son back? What brings any lost person back? What brought you back? What brought me back? Emptiness? Was it loneliness? Homesickness? Is it the memory of a mother and father's love?

The younger son had two gifts going for him. He was gifted with *family,* and he was gifted with the ability to *dream.*

He has a father. The great word for God as far as Jesus is concerned is Father!
Jesus will never let us forget his Father. There is no sermon in which Father does not appear. There is no prayer of Jesus in which Father is missing. The first record of Jesus
speaking is, "Did you not know that I must be in my Father's house?
The last word on the cross is, "Father, into your hands, I commend my spirit."

Does the son in the parable have a living mother? We do not know. Author Henri Nouwen sees in Rembrandt's famous painting *Return of the Prodigal,* (Hermitage Museum in St. Petersburg) the right hand of the father on the son's shoulder as feminine, suggesting that God as Father and Mother both are present.

When Jesus wants to tell the world what God is like, he takes this word "Father" and weaves it into an incomparable unforgettable family story. "There was a man, (a father)
who had two sons..."

The younger son is also gifted to *dream.*
His heart's hungry for happiness
His imagination thirsts for excitement.
He yearns for freedom.
He dreams of an adventurous life.

Take the *dreamers* out of the world and life gets mighty dull.
Prophets dream *dreams* and see a new Israel.
Martin Luther King *dreams "I Have A Dream"* and a new societal vision bursts forth.
Johnny Appleseed *dreams* and barren land sprouts lovely apple orchards.
My friend Ed Yost *dreams* the possibility of inventing a modern hot air balloon.
And because of Ed's dream and modern invention, tens of thousands of hot air balloons adorn the skies throughout the earth.

"Every great advance in history," said, Dr. Whitehead, "has issued from a new audacity in imagination."

But not all dreams can be trusted. Think of the dashed dreams in Las Vegas and Deadwood. One day this father's son had a dream, but it turned out to be a deception – a nightmare. It was an image in the son's mind that had no existence in reality.

Our night dreams are full of that when the mind is free of inhibitions. Our night dreams paint strange fiction on the screen. Day dreams too, deceive us. We imagine things, to be even when they aren't so.

My wife Pam and I had a dream. We went to Murfreesboro, Arkansas to *Crater of Diamonds State Park.* There we dug for diamonds in the soft dirt they plow up for tourists. We dug and dug. We walked away tired, disappointed with only a couple of colored, worthless stones.

Dreams are elusive. A little boy, playing on the lawn, saw a butterfly flit from flower to flower. He watched, fascinated by its graceful beauty. How fun it would be to catch it and keep it. So when the butterfly lighted softly on a flower petal he sneaked up and grabbed it. But then he found he didn't have it at all. All he had in his open hand was an ugly smear and a crushed skeleton of wings.

We know Jesus story. We know the ending. One day that younger son came to himself. He went back home. Thank God for sadness. This sadness is the sign of sonship; it is God's everlasting whisper in the human heart. One might think sadness, discontent and restlessness are signs that God is far away. On the contrary, sadness and yearning are the sure signs of God's close presence.

When Leo Tolstoy, the great Russian author of *War and Peace, Anna Karenina, The Cossacks* and *Resurrection,* was about fifty he felt life was going stale. For two years he went through a period of mental torture. Life had no meaning. Life was futile and empty, not worth the struggle. He hid rope lest he hang himself. He wouldn't carry a gun into the forest lest he shoot himself. Life lost its purpose.

One day, walking in the forest alone, Tolstoy got to thinking about God and found himself wondering why he should. There was an up rush of hope in him.
Suddenly he felt stable and secure. Life took on a new meaning. "This is it," he said, "I will seek God and live." (Source unknown)

"This is the life," said Jesus, "I came that you may have life and have life abundantly"
(John 10:10b).

It is not easy to come back. Ask any alcoholic, drug addict, former boxing champions, a prodigal child. The comeback trail is tough.
But the young son did come back. And so can our sons and daughters – so can you and I.

Amen.

Week Two

"DAD, I'M LEAVING"

Talking Hats
(Children's Mission Minute)

Props: Hats, Caps, and various Lids
Setting: Imagining a hat that talks – and oh, the story it tells

Mission Minute Two

Hello Boys and Girls,

Have you heard of Talking Hats?
Talking Hats is a let's pretend hats talk. We call it our Mission Minute for kids.
Remember last week we met a *Happy* Talking Hat? He/she was a cowboy/cowgirl hat with a brim turned up like a smiley face.

Today, I am wearing a fisherman's hat. See the brim turned downward like a sad sack face.

Jesus told a story about sadness. The story, which we call a parable, is about a boy who wore a sad sack face. The boy wanted to be glad but ended up sad. The boy left his father's home, headed out for a faraway country and ended up living a bad, sad life.

He got sad because he was hungry. He was lonesome. He was tired out. He had no true friends. I am sure his father was very sad too when his son left home.

So let's talk to the Fisherman's Hat.
Hello Sad Hat.

Sad Hat: *"Hi boys and girls. We like to be glad but sometimes we get sad like me.*
You know it is okay to be sad once in a while – now and then. Life is that way.
You know what? God loves us even when we are sad besides when we are glad and when we are mad and when we are bad.

Does God love us all the time no matter how we feel?

Sad Hat: *You bet! God's love never quits!*

Wow! That's awesome!

Sad Hat: *"Sad things happen all the time like when our friends move away. Sad like when your puppy gets sick. Sad like when you get hurt or sick. It's okay to cry.*
Jesus cried when his good friend Lazarus died. Jesus cried because he loved Lararus so much.

Mr./Ms. Fisherman's Hat, when I see sad friends and sometimes they are crying – what can I do?

Sad Hat: *Lots! Just listen to sad people. Be a friend. Give them your love and attention.*
Don't blab a lot. Be quiet. Pray for them. Pray with them.

Will they be glad?

Sad Hat: *Yes, yes. They will be glad indeed – just like the boy who came home in Jesus'*
parable – and everybody was glad!

Thanks for visiting with us today Fisherman's Sad Hat.
Now boys and girls let us pray.

Lord Jesus, thank you for being you – a real person who sometimes got sad. Thank you for loving us no matter how we feel. You love us when we are mad or glad or sad and even when we are bad. Thank you for forgiveness and the chance to always come back to you.
Amen.

Leaving Home
(A chancel drama)

Setting/situation: Mom and Dad discuss their feelings when each of their three children left home – a career son, a runaway daughter, and a soldier.

Scene: Center stage at a table

Players: Mom – Gladys, dad - Homer, son - Jim, daughter - Lola, son - Lance

Gladys: Next week is our wedding anniversary Homer. Can you believe it?

Homer: Seems like yesterday. Time sure flies.

Gladys: When we're having fun??

Homer: (laughs) Yeah – some of the time.
Really Gladys it's been quite a ride! Our marriage that is. We've had our ups and downs – of course. Mostly ups.

Gladys: Sure have. Went best when I got my way. (laughs)

Homer: Remember when each of our kids left home?

Gladys: Do I? I cried every time.

Homer: Remember when Jim left for college and then went on to medical school?

Gladys: Yes I do. And as we often said, it seems like yesterday.

(Homer and Gladys freeze)

Jim: (stage right) I'm all packed Mom and Dad. Car is filled with gas.
Think the old Buick will make Northfield? St. Olaf here I come!
Yahoo! Bye. See you at Thanksgiving break – love you! (leaves)

(Homer and Gladys unfreeze)

Gladys: Yes, that was almost twenty years ago. My goodness.

Homer: Seems like yesterday. That old Buick made it.

Gladys: Of course I cried when Jim left. Shouldn't have I suppose. But couldn't help crying – I suppose both tears of sadness and joy – our eldest son off to college – first to leave the nest.

Homer: Remember when Lola left?

Gladys: Do I? Do I? Oh my!

Homer: That was hard especially when she was so young.

Gladys: Yes, only sixteen.

Homer: Too young, way too young. Troubled in school, bad friends and.....

        (Homer and Gladys freeze)

Lola: (stage left) (angrily) Mom, Dad, I've had it! You're always, always ruling
            and controlling me. Your rules, your unfair demands – I have to be home by
            midnight and all my friends don't have to. I hate you! You are the worst
            parents ever – I'm leaving. I'm going far away — ah maybe to Las Vegas. Good bye.
            (slams door and leaves noisily)

        (Homer and Gladys unfreeze)

Gladys: Oh, that was a terrible night. That was the last time we heard from Lola – nearly
            two years ago. I wonder if she's okay. I wonder what she's doing. Wonder if
            she's happy. I pray to God every night for my dear little Lola. I pray for her
            safety and about her addictions – oh God help us.

Homer: Breaks my heart. She was my sweet little daughter and then what happened? Hope
            she comes home someday.

Gladys: Remember when Lance left for Afghanistan?

Homer: Sure do.

Gladys: So far away. It was so dangerous even though he was assigned as a medic.

Homer: I'll never forget seeing him get on the plane and waving good bye.
            Seems like only yesterday.

        (Homer and Gladys freeze)

Lance: (in uniform state right) Bye mom, bye dad. They just told me I'm deployed for Kabul.
            I'll be fine. See you when my deployment is done. (leaves)

        (Homer and Gladys unfreeze)

Homer: Yep, they go one by one. Some in honor. Some not so good. Like all
            parents it's so hard to see our children leave. Some for bright careers, others for the
            streets of who knows what, some for patriotic duty serving their country. Always we
            parents grieve and pray and hope one day they will return home. We yearn like the
            yearning in Emmylou Harris' song *Calling My Children Home.*

Gladys: Our kids - we love them forever. Hope they are around for our fortieth!

On Leaving
(A Message)

Do you remember the first time you left home? Or better yet, recall the first time your son or daughter left home. Remember the circumstances? How did you feel? For some it was a relief. For most it was hard.

I remember dropping off my younger daughter, Rebekah, at Augustana University.
We were happy for her, but there was a lump in my throat as we drove away.
And that's the way it works – our children go away to college, to trade school, to serve in the armed forces, or to a distant place to work.

Today our series exploring Jesus' parable, entitled, *A Long, Long Road Back To Love,* is about coming home – homecoming.
Home coming produces joy.
Home leaving produces immense sorrow.

We see scenes of home leaving at bus terminals, at airports. We see tears flow as spouses and children say good bye as their soldier heads for Afghanistan.

Jesus' story tells it simply, "So a few days later the younger son gathers all he has and travels to a distant country."

But this home leaving was hardly a lad jumping on his Harley and speeding off to the Sturgis Rally for the weekend.
It was a death wish for his father! To request one's share of the family wealth while his father was still alive, was to wish him dead!

Kenneth Bailey, in his research in *The Cross and the Prodigal,* pointed out that every Middle-Eastern peasant understands this parable instinctively. Bailey wrote, "With endless village groups across the Middle East, I have tested this...this request meant he wanted his father to die!"

The son's home leaving was an offense.
His home leaving was a heartless rejection. It was a break with tradition. It was a betrayal of the treasured values of family and community. It was a broken relationship. Though he had not broken an Old Testament law (Deuteronomy 21:17 stated that the younger son's portion was one third) the tragedy of the son's leaving shows that he had become deaf to the voice of love. It was the same voice that spoke from the clouds centuries later when it said to Jesus, "You are my beloved, on you my favor dwells."

The younger son saw the glitter, the glamour, and the neon lights of the distant country.
He left his true home and found a borrowed home.
The prodigal is like Carlo Collodi's classic *Pinocchio.* In an updated paraphrase, Pinocchio and his two friends sang this song when they arrived in their own distant country – the *Land of the Toys:*
"Here we are and we all agree,
there's no happier place to be…"
But the Land of the Toys turned out to be less than wonderful.

Soon Pinocchio was lamenting about that just when he began to feel strong, everything would go wrong....and he felt as if he would be better off at the bottom of the sea.

Leaving can lead to choices both "wrong and foolish." The Greek in the New Revised Standard Version is a rare word – *asotos*. The meaning is clear. It means "foolish." A person who is wise and makes good choices is *sotos*. One example of *sotos* might be applied to Joseph in the book of Genesis.

In Jesus' parable, the son was one who was foolish and made bad choices. He was *asotos*.

Home leaving for some is faith leaving.
My uncle Gustave moved to Seattle from the midwest in the 1950's for work at Boeing.
I remember once he spun this metaphor – he said that the Cascade Mountains were white when you pass over them – not white with snow but with the letters of church transfers tossed out the window when midwesterners went west. It has been said that Washington State was the most unchurched state in the lower 48 at that time and may still win a nomination if not the Oscar for church leaving today.

Church leaving today is dramatized by the rapid and growing number of those whose religious affiliation is designated as "none" or "done." Many say they are spiritual, but not religious. Is this a mixed blessing/curse?

Now the distant country is not a *place*, but a *space*. It is a space in our relationships with God and with one another. It is a space in one's inner life.

The distant country infected me like a virus my sophomore year at college in Parkland, Washington. I was not living a desolate life of drunkenness, carousing, and promiscuity, but living rather an overly dedicated life and I was exhausted. I worked three jobs while maintaining a full academic schedule. My social life was zero. I began to feel a space in my heart and my emotions. I began to feel disconnected from my body – almost an out of body sensation. "It's time to check in with Chaplain Lutnes," I said to myself. Then my dear older brother, Marlowe, showed up for a day visit. I left all my obligations behind. It was like an intervention. We simply went downtown Tacoma, shopped, explored, ate and talked. Those eight hours together became Sabbath for me. It became a miraculous time of renewal, rest and revitalization. I have never forgotten that weird experience all these later years, as it truly became the healing of a space in my inner life.

Sabbath repairs that space. Sabbath fills the void. Does your life need sabbath? Are you tired? Angry? Lonely? Make sabbath. Receive sabbath by the grace and love of God.

My sister Oriette made sabbath from time to time by traveling to Blue Cloud Abbey at Marvin, South Dakota for a spiritual renewal. Her space was filled. She would come back home forgiven, refreshed, and renewed.

The distant country is not necessarily a place, but truly a space.

It is amazing that Adam and Eve and all their rebellious descendants are forgiven.
And herein lies the mystery of life and faith. You and I are loved so much that we are given freedom.
We are given the only affirmation we need and that voice is saying not only to Jesus at his baptism and transfiguration, but to you and to me. "You are my beloved, on you my favor rests."

When we leave home and head for the Land of the Toys – we can come home.
Some do. Some don't.

Amen.

Week Three

"DAD/MOM, I MISS YOU"

Talking Hats
(Children's Mission Minute)

Props: Hats, Caps, and various Lids
Setting: Imagining a hat that talks – and oh, the story it tells

Mission Minute Three

Hello Boys and Girls,

Look at what I am wearing today. What is it?

Yes, it's called a hard hat or a construction hat.
Construction workers wear this special hard hat to protect their heads from injury.
A branch or a piece of wood or a rock could fall from above and "boink!"
No need to worry on the job when one wears this good friend – Hard Hat.

Since we are pretending our hats can talk in this Talking Hats mission minute let's see what Hard Hat has to say to us.

Hard Hat: *"Hello boys and girls. Come feel how hard my hat is.* (kids touch the hard hat and may even put it on briefly)
People wear me when they are busy building something or fixing something.
They wear me when they build houses and apartments and bridges and roads.

I especially love being worn by people who build homes for families who have limited income and for the homeless.

Are there kids and moms and dads who need shelter and their own place to live?

Hard Hat: *"Oh yes! Some folks end up, because of difficulties in their lives – living in cars, under bridges and in cardboard refrigerator boxes. Homeless people are often cold and hungry and unhappy.*
And you know what? People loved by God and who love others build homes for the homeless and for families with limited income through an organization called **Habitat for Humanity.**
Can you say that? Haaa biii ttaat for Huuu man iiit yyy. (kids repeat)
Good you got it.

(Hard Hat tells a bit about Habitat's mission especially if a project is being built in the area)

You mean homeless moms, dads, kids, and future homeowners who help the builders, can get a home and get out of the cold weather and hot sun?

Hard Hat: *Oh yes, that is the beauty of God's love seen in people who wear me – helping others. With hammers, tape measures, and chop saws, protected by me, they go to work. In no time, a house is built, and a homeless family, or a family with limited income, at last, has a place to live.*

Is there some way we can be builders too?

Hard Hat: *Sure. Right now we can begin to help. So let's play "pass the hard hat."*

How does "pass the hard hat work?"

Hard Hat: *"We will take up a special offering for the homeless and those with limited income. Instead of passing me around like a collection plate, let's pass this tin can around. We'll call this a 'noisy offering.' When coins are dropped in the tin can they make a beautiful noise – clink, clang, bang. And the more clinks, clangs, and bangs – the better.*

(Children run around and pick up donations of coins and paper money)

Let us pray:
Lord Jesus in your mercy and love you care for all people – especially the homeless, the lost and the lonely. Use our hands and hearts for building shelters for and with others.
Amen.

The Great Discovery
(A chancel drama)

Synopsis: Several people tell the story of a personal spiritual epiphany.
                    Each gives testimony of their personal insight, discovery, rebirth, and new
   life.

Characters: (In costume when possible and appropriate)
                    Farmer in Jesus' Parable (Matthew 13:44)
                    Alexander Fleming
                    Martin Luther
                    John Wesley
                    C.S. Lewis
                    Lee Strobel
                    Nadia Bolz-Weber (cf. Book *Pastrix* published by Jericho books)
                    Personal witnesses from the community

Farmer in Jesus' parable

Hello. I am the farmer in one of Jesus' powerful parables. I went out plowing one day in one of my fields. It was a hot day, a tiring day. Up and down, down and up the furrows I walked. It was monotonous to be sure. Then it happened! All of a sudden I heard the clink of metal on my plowshare. Should I keep going or should I stop?

I stopped. I dug into the soft sandy dirt as quickly as I could with my bare hands. And would you know? There it was! Buried treasure! Oh my. Surprise. Surprise.

Alexander Fleming

Hello. I am Alexander Fleming. I was a botanist. I lived in Scotland and in London. You may not recall my name but I believe you will recognize my amazing discovery. Here's what happened. I was working in my laboratory, when looking carefully in a petri dish, I spied a clean area ringing with contamination. Microbes had approached the contamination area and appeared to be dissolved by it – thereby enlarging the clean area. You know what? I discovered penicillin. The miracle antibiotic drug. What a find. What a fantastic discovery – and now you know the rest of the story.

Martin Luther

Guten tag. Good day. I am Martin Luther. You know my story and why I am here today. I was tormented for a long time about the status of my soul. I worried that I could not do enough good works to save my soul. Then one day, as I studied scriptures, I realized that the "just live by faith." Oh my. I realized that it is by the grace of God grasped by faith by which I am saved.

I exploded with an epiphany. It was neither my pilgrimages to Rome nor my self-flagellation in the monastery that satisfied the justice of God. It was God's saving grace in Jesus that changed my life. Praise God.

John Wesley

Hello. I am John Wesley the founder of the Methodist Church.
Here's what happened to me. It was May 24, 1734, that I had a transforming experience. I was at an Anglican Society meeting in Aldersgate Street in London.
We were reading Martin Luther's *Preface to the Commentary of Romans*.
About a quarter before nine, while Luther was describing the change which God works in

the heart through faith in Christ, *I felt my heart strangely warmed.*

I felt I did trust Christ – Christ alone for salvation and an assurance was given me, that Christ had taken away my sins...and saved me from the law of sin and death.

My brother, Charles Wesley, had experienced a similar conversion only three days earlier on May 21. Thanks be to God.

C.S. Lewis

My name is Clive Staples Lewis. Just call me C.S. I was an agnostic until I became a Christian. Later as a new Christian, in 1952, I wrote a book that became a classic in Christian Apologetics, titled *Mere Christianity*.

Here's one thing I said:

"I am trying here to prevent anyone saying the really foolish thing that people often say about him (Christ): they say,'I'm ready to accept Jesus as a great moral teacher, but I don't accept his claim to be God.....a man who was merely a man and said the sort of things Jesus said would not be a great moral teacher. He would be either a lunatic—on the level with the man who says he is a poached egg – or else he would be the devil of hell. You must make your choice. Either this man was and is the Son of God: or else a madman or a demon.' Make your choice. I did. (*Mere Christianity* p. 41 The MacMillan Company, 1960)

Lee Strobel

Hello. My name is Lee Strobel from Illinois. I wrote the book *The Case for Christ*. For much of my life I was a skeptic. In fact I considered myself an atheist. To me there's far too much evidence that God was merely a product of wishful thinking, of ancient mythology or primitive superstition. How could there be a loving God? What about miracles? Doesn't scientific reasoning dispel belief in the supernatural?

So I launched an all-out investigation into the facts surrounding the case for Christianity. After an intense search – the atheism I had embraced for so long buckled under the weight of historic truth. It was a stunning and radical outcome. I trusted Jesus as the Son of God and my Savior. Wow. What a trip! I now write and lecture across the land. (Paraphrased from Lee Strobel's *The Case for Christ* published by Zondervan, 1998)

Nadua Bolz-Weber

My name is Nadia. I have only my confession — confession of my own real brokeness and confession of my own real faith to offer … my story is about the development of my faith, the expression of my faith, and the community of my faith. And it is the story of how I have experienced this Jesus thing to be true. How the Christian faith, while wildly misrepresented in so much of American culture, is really about the death and resurrection. It is about how God continues to reach into the graves we dig for oursleves and pull us out, giving us new life, in ways both dramatic and small. (Heavily tattooed and loud-mouthed, Nadia a former stand-up comic… didn't consider herself to be religious leader material — until the day she ended up leading a friend's funeral in a smoky downtown (Denver) comedy club. Surrounded by fellow alcoholics, depressives, and cynics, she realized: These were her people. Maybe she was meant to be their pastor.) (Quote from book cover of Pastrix)

A Contemporary Witnesses from your community

Narrator: You have just heard from some folks who have experienced a dramatic discovery in their lives. Change happens by the grace and power of God.

Living In And Leaving The Distant Country
(A Message)

Luke 15:14b-18a

When the younger son landed in the distant country, he quickly got lost. And in his *lostness* he forgot who he was. He forgot his father had said,"everything I have is yours." He forgot he was the "beloved on whom the father dwells and loves."
 He forgot. He failed to remember his childhood catechism like the psalms he had sung with family and community. Only later could he identify with Psalm 119: "I have gone astray like a lost sheep."

At first the younger son had no knowledge that he was lost, like the little girl who went to a large rally with her parents. The auditorium was crowded and she got lost. The master of ceremonies announced after a time: "A little Mary Jones is lost. Her family is worried. If anyone has seen her, please go to the door and tell her parents." At the close of the meeting when the people were leaving, a lady noticed little Mary sitting in the front row. She leaned over and asked, "Mary, didn't you hear the man asking about you? Why didn't you let them know you were here?"

Surprised, Mary said, "Did they mean me? They said Mary Jones was lost. I'm not lost.
I knew where I was all the time. I thought it was some other Mary Jones." (Seeds from the Sower by Michael Guido)

The younger son, unaware that he was lost, lived recklessly and squandered his resources.
He got hungry. He was empty. Loneliness set in. Lost people quickly get lonely. He sang like Bono in his rock band U2, "I still haven't found what I'm looking for."

Henri Nouwen says it is important to learn to move from a "first loneliness" to a "second loneliness." "The first loneliness is the emotional loneliness; you need friends, you need family, you need home. But when you satisfy all those needs you have to suddenly learn that there is another loneliness. God is calling you to deep personal intimacy. You must say, 'Yes, I am lonely for I know that this loneliness pushes me to know personally, the true God."

Oh the games people play. We do our best to please others so we may get their approval. When I fail, I feel jealous of those who succeed. When I succeed, I worry that others will be jealous or resentful of me. I fear that I have nothing to give to others. And if I have nothing to give then I might be abandoned, rejected and ultimately lost.

I heard Professor Jim Nestingen, then of Luther Seminary, say in a lecture, "if you don't believe in original sin, just listen to country western music." Country western music is about loss and loneliness. I lost my love. I lost my dog. I lost my pick up. I've lost my way.

Professor Jim Fillingham who teaches ethics and biblical studies at Chowan College in Murfreesboro, North Carolina once asked, "What can country music teach us about Christian ethics? What can I learn from Hank Williams?"

Still appearing in classic country western lore is Hank William's *Jambayla (On the Bayou)* and *"craw fish pie and fillet gumbo"* and *Wealth Won't Save Your Soul,* and *Your Cheatin' Heart Will Tell On You,"* makes it clear – actions have consequences. (see the lyrics to *Your Cheatin' Heart*)

We are responsible for our actions and our choices. Responding to life's troubles and/or successes escaping in drugs, booze, sex, and/or hedonism only brings more trouble. One ends up with a "cheatin' heart" or like George Jone's "still doing time in a honky-tonky prison." Despite the fact that humans are "born to trouble as sparks fly upward" (Job 7:5), we are responsible for our choices. Someone said, "our best bet, since none of us will get out of this world alive, is to join hands with some friends in low places and work together for justice." Then, "son of a gun, we'll have big fun," and not only "on the bayou" like Hank.

On the door of a church in London is this sign: "Not everyone who attends this church is converted. Please watch your handbags."

When the dark voices of my surroundings try to persuade me that I am no good and that I can only become good by earning my goodness, those voices lead me quickly to forget the voice that calls you and me, "my son, my child, the beloved."

"And the younger son came to himself." Herein lies the miracle of the heart. The Holy Spirit speaks and acts. The son receives a spark of enlightenment – an epiphany, "how many of my father's hired men have all the food they want and more, and here I am dying of hunger – I will return!"

The miracle in the heart and mind is to come alive – like when Saul became Paul on the road to Damascus (Acts 9). Repentance is to come to your senses

Robert Chambers, Scotch scientist, born 1802, said the greatest day in his life was the day when he found an old copy of Encyclopedia Britannica in his attic: for up to that day he never realized there was any such thing as geology or astronomy. He said it was like opening of a window in a prison through which for the first time he saw the world.

An epiphany happens whenever I experience an event and say, "I get it."
Horace Bushnell, pastor and theologian in the 1800's leaped out of bed one night, seeing for the first time what he had been taught from childhood. "I see it," he said, "I have found it. I have found the gospel." A new life began for him in that moment of insight.

He saw reality for the first time in what he had known all his life.

The core epiphany, understood in Christian teachings, motivated by grace, often begins with "I have found it" and ends with the greater insight, "it has found me."

A man went to a Billy Graham crusade and sat next to a medical doctor. They chatted for a time before the service expressing their doubts about the charade. Nonetheless, Evangelist Billy Graham preached a powerful sermon with an invitation to come forward and receive Christ. Suddenly the doctor got up from his chair and then turned to the stranger sitting next to him and said, "I'm going forward." The man sitting next to the doctor got up too and said, "I'm going up too – here's your wallet. I am a pick pocket." (source unknown)

The transformative power of grace is at work.

The New York Times best seller, *Pastrix,* described as a "cranky, beautiful faith of a sinner/saint," reveals the story of Nadia Bolz-Weber's spiritual journey. Nadia, a "heavily tattooed, former loud mouth comic, didn't regard herself as a religious leader – until the day she ended up leading a friend's funeral surrounded by fellow alcoholics, depressives, and cynics." Today Nadia is an Evangelical Lutheran Church in America pastor who formerly served *Sinners and Saints Church* in Denver, Colorado.

My former colleague in ministry, Pastor Dave, tells when he was in his twenties he either lived by the rules (law) or rebelled against the rules in his faith journey. One day sitting in a Lutheran church, which was not his denominational upbringing, he heard a message say, "rules didn't matter." He heard, "Jesus kept the rules for me and I am free."

Dave said, " I still fall back into old patterns but now I know that the law kills and Christ makes alive."

The younger son said "I will get up and go to my father." And he did! And by the Holy Spirit at work in us – so can you and so can I.

Amen.

Week Four

"I'M COMING HOME"

TALKING HATS
(Children's Mission Minute)

Props: Hats, Caps, and various Lids
Setting: Imagining a hat that talks – and oh, the story it tells

Mission Minute Four

Hello Boys and Girls,

Notice the hat I'm wearing! (wears a colorful stocking cap)
Do you know what you call a hat like this? (shows stocking cap with a flourish)
You're right it's a Stocking Cap.

I love wearing this Stocking Cap especially when a cold north wind blows.
When the temperature drops this Stocking Cap pops out of its hiding place and plops right on my head.
(puts cap back on head)
Oooh, ah, that feels soooo gooood!

Now I'm going to let you in on a little secret. Know what? Stocky here, can talk.
He talks just as much as your imagination will allow.

(takes off cap and makes it talk)

Would you like to talk to Stocky?

Hi, Stocky. You look so colorful and warm and cozy. How did you get to be that way?

Stocky Cap: "Well boys and girls, yarn, wool, and dye spun together with lots a love made me what I am. My job is to bring warmth and coziness to kids and moms and dads when it's cold. Sometimes people with cancer wear me when they lose their hair.
You know, if I had lived in Jesus' day, I would gladly have given myself to that lost boy in Jesus' parable. That boy must have been not only lonely and hungry but cold too."

Yes, that's an amazing parable about that boy who left home and who almost never returned home.

I agree, Stocky, that boy shivering, must have remembered his father and mother's warm home with cozy blankets and hot chocolate. I'll bet that's one reason he did finally came home.

43

Stocky Cap: "I love bringing warmth and coziness to all God's children."

What else do you do today, Stocky ?

Stocky Cap: "Pretend when you put me on you are putting on warm things like forgiveness and love and acceptance of others.

Wow! I like that!

Stocky Cap: "I have friends who do the same thing I do. They bring warmth and coziness too.

Well, who are they Stocky?

Stocky Cap: "My friend Mitten. My friend Socks. My friends Gloves, Clothes, Blankets, and Quilts.

Oh my. So many wonderful friends. You know you and your friends are badly needed right now. Whenever you and your friends give yourselves to the homeless and sick and lonely, you are like giving a person in need, God's love and compassion.

Stocky Cap: "That's my passion. Oh I see somebody who needs me. Gotta go. Bye now.
(cap goes back on head)

Let's pray,
Lord Jesus thank you for Stocky and his friends and for all the gifts Stocky brings of warmth and kindness to the needy.
Amen.

How Will Dad React?
(A Chancel drama)

Character: Disheveled sixteen-year-old lad
(Music)

Lad: Oh no, am I in trouble! Took Dad's car without asking him and then – idiot me – decided to give the Lexus a good old Nascar run. Does that Lexus have guts? Smooth machine! Wow! (sits down, gets up, sits down nervously)

I can just imagine the police report: *"Ah, ah this is Officer O'Malley from the 9th precinct. It appears a young lad took his father's 2020 silver Lexus, license number 21-666, for a spin without permission from either his mother or father, spun out of control and hit a parked semi-truck.*

There are no fatalities in fact no one was seriously injured.

I will continue the investigation. Yes, I'm checking on the young man's driver's license, insurance coverage, and then......."

I just got my driver's permit last week. Did okay in driver's ed ... but I guess I got distracted when I dropped my smart phone and tried to pick it up ... and then there was this semi-truck right in front of me. Where did he come from?
Oh, I guess he was parked.

I wonder what Dad will say? I wonder what Dad will do?
(paces up and down stage)
Let's see, he could ground me for the next ten years. Or make me work at the warehouse the rest of my life. Or never let me drive again. Or maybe he'll be glad I'm not injured and alive and might just say, "Ah shucks son, I was a kid once too and..."
Or if he was a violent Dad (which thankfully he is not) he might give me a lickin'
or maybe a scolding ... or I don't know what he's going to do.

I sure deserve punishment but I love my Dad and my Dad loves me, maybe,
maybe, just maybe....

(music)

Coming Home
(A Message)

Luke 15:18-21 "I will get up and go to my father and say to him, 'Father I have sinned against heaven and before you; I am no longer worthy to be called your son; treat me like one of your hired hands." So he set off and went to his father. But while he was still far off, his father saw him and was filled with compassion; he ran and put his arms around him and kissed him. Then the son said to him, 'Father, I have sinned against heaven and before you; I am no longer worthy to be called your son.'"

What was it that finally brought the son back home to his father?
What brought him to the point of confession, hardly hoping for forgiveness and acceptance? Did he remember the sorrow of his father?
Did he remember the laments and longings in his father's heart?

The father could well have sung the words to "O Danny Boy."(in the public domain)

> But come ye back when summer's in the meadow
> or when the valley's hushed and white with snow
> 'tis I'll be there in sunshine or shadow,
> Oh Danny boy, oh Danny boy, I love you so.

When our children leave home in rebellion or boredom or disgust, the loving parent prays and hopes.

Jim Cress in "Ministry" magazine, wrote an article titled "PK Prodigals", in which he laments, "many clergy parents are overwhelmed with anger, guilt, shame, self-condemnation, and resentment when their PK's (preacher's kids), depart their upbringing.
God seems to have failed God's own work. After all doesn't the Bible promise, 'train up a child in the way he should go and when he is old, he will not depart from it?" (Proverbs 22:6).

Emmylou Harris in her CD *Heartaches and Highways* plaintively expressed the pained heart of a parent: (written by Doyle Lawson, Charles Walker and Robert Yates' - listen also to Chanticleer's touching rendition of this song.) She pondered on whether those children would one day return and expressed her loneliness for them.
Some come back and some do not.

The late Keith Miller, (author of books such as *The Taste of New Wine, Second Touch*) worried constantly about his daughters. One day he began to pray a different prayer each morning. "Instead of talking to God about each child's needs, I stated imagining that I was placing each one, one at a time in my cupped hands. I would imagine being before God. God also had cupped hands. I would place my hands inside God's hands and gently take my hands apart, leaving each daughter in God's hands. I didn't say anything, but just released them to God. And just this one act seemed to take the pressure off me to run my girls' lives...."

It is not easy to come back. Talk to an ex-convict. Ask any beaten athlete from blind Samson to Mohammed Ali. The true story of boxer, Jim Braddock, in the *Cinderella Man* movie, is a prime example. For the love of his family, Jim Braddock drove himself relentlessly, until he won the heavyweight boxing title of the world in the 1930's. He had lost several bouts due to chronic hand injury. He was forced to work on the docks to strengthen his hands and make a living for his family. He lived in part on social assistance to support his family during the depression. Then in 1935, he fought Max Baer for the Heavyweight Championship, and won!

It is not easy to come back and face family and community.

Yet, it is possible to come back. It is possible to make a comeback and win.
The son did come back.

And it is not easy to confess, "I have sinned against heaven and against you my father."
"He admitted," says Henri Nouwen, "that he was unable to make it on his own and confessed that he would get better treatment not as a son, but as a hired hand. He knew that he was still the son, but he told himself that he had lost the dignity to be called 'son' and so prepared himself to accept the status of a 'hired man.' There is repentance, but not repentance in the light of the immense love of a forgiving God. It is a self-serving repentance that offers the possibility of survival."

How many of us discover we can't make it on our own and go to God and ask for forgiveness in the hope that one will receive a minimal punishment? Does God remain a harsh, judgmental God? Seeing God like this makes one feel guilty and resentful.

One of the greatest challenges of the spiritual life is to receive God's forgiveness.
There is something in us humans that keeps clinging to our sins.
We block God deleting our past and offering a new beginning.

Receiving forgiveness is a gift. It comes as an epiphany when we suddenly blurt out, "I get it."
As a hired hand I can still keep my distance, complain, and reject the father. As a beloved son/daughter, washed clean, you and I get to claim our full dignity and potential.

Near the end of his life, Mickey Mantle, baseball great, received a liver transplant after years of alcohol abuse. Mickey Mantle told the media: "You talk about role models. This is your role model – don't be like me."

However in the ninth inning of life, Mickey Mantle hit a personal home run. He pleaded eloquently with others to take heed of his mistakes. Even saying, "Don't be like me," and
fans new and old, in his final days, showered him with an outpouring of love.

The father's forgiveness is unconditional.

We are more accustomed to "conditional forgiveness."
Two sisters feuded all their lives. Hilda became ill and went to the hospital.
Sister Frieda visited her. Since Hilda was gravely ill, Frieda told her she forgave her all their disagreements and fights. But Frieda added, "Hilda, if you get better, then things stay the same."

Unconditional forgiveness flows from the cross. Jesus covers all sins without reservation. To confess, "I have sinned," is the doorway to new life.

Little did the son know that the father stood on tiptoe every day peering down the dusty road hoping that the day would come. Then one day it came.

Nearly 125 years ago, a Roman Catholic magazine in England published a poem by an unknown poet. The poet, two years before, had been a drunken, destitute drug addict.

His name was Francis Thompson and his poem, "The Hound of Heaven" had these words:
"I fled him down the nights and down the days; I fled him down the arches of the years; I fled him down the labyrinthine ways, of my own mind; and in the midst of tears I hid from him and running laughter....from those strong feet that followed, followed after."(in the public domain)

No one thought it was much of a poem. No one thought it would amount to anything, but "The Hound of Heaven" by Francis Thompson has been translated into more than sixty languages and as the *New York Times* said in an editorial, "It is one of the few English lyrics that makes the same powerful appeal to all nationalities and faiths."

American poet Robert Frost, as a young aspiring poet, found a copy of it in a Massachusetts book store and spent his last carfare money to buy it.
Playwright Eugene O'Neil memorized it; he knew every one of its 183 lines by heart.

"The Hound of Heaven" is a poem about our seeking God "whose strong feet followed, followed after."

The Father in Jesus' parable seeks, waits, and forgives. His are the "strong feet followed, followed after."

Cal, a member of a church I served in the Black Hills of South Dakota faced open heart surgery. Just before surgery he told me his story:
"I was an atheist for thirty years. I hated God and God's people."

Cal was a Harley man. He loved his motorcycle but despised and cursed those Christian motorcyclists that came up to the Sturgis rally every August. "One night," Cal told me,
"I deliberately drove my "HOG" right through a group as they stood in a discussion and prayer circle. I knocked down one tall blond guy, a member of the Association of Riders of the Son. That tall blond guy got up from the ground and went over to me and gave me a hug and said, "I love you brother."

One day it came to this. Cal was drunk. He had a pistol in one hand and a fifth of whiskey in the other. He stumbled into the Little White Church in Hill City, South Dakota. The secretary heard a noise. She went into the sanctuary and saw Cal.

She called the pastor. The pastor came. He took Cal's gun and bottle and told him to go home. Then the pastor told Cal to come back in four hours. Cal did. The miracle began.
Cal gave up hubris (pride) and surrendered his life to God.

"I am the happiest man in the world," he told me as he faced his upcoming surgery.
Then he added, "I wish to God I could find that tall blond guy and tell him I'm sorry. I'll find him someday."

All we like sheep have gone astray.
The Father is waiting.

Amen.

Week Five

"PARTY TIME!"

TALKING HATS
(Children's Mission Minute)

Props: Hats, Caps, and various Lids
Setting: Imagining a hat that talks – and oh, the story it tells

<u>*Mission Minute Five*</u>

Hello Boys and Girls,

Today I'm wearing a Dr. Seuss Hat. Like it?

(Google "make a Dr. Seuss paper hat" for instructions for the following)
     Option #1 – "I have made a Dr. Seuss hat for each of you. Here put it on."
     Option #2 – "Here's how to make a Dr. Seuss hat." (Actually make one)
     Option #3 – (Simply talk about your hat)

Now why in the world should you and I wear this funny, silly hat?
After all, there's no bat in the hat.
There's no rat in the hat.
There's no cat in the hat.
No nat. No vat.

Let's ask Dr. Seuss' Hat, since, did you know, he/she is a talking hat?

Why should we wear this hat today? (Take hat off and manipulate as a puppet)

Dr. Seuss Hat: (talking) *"Hi boys and girls. Dr. Seuss Hat here. Yes, yes, I am a wacky, smacky, tacky, talking Hat. And you know what? Once I almost ate green eggs and ham.*
Do you remember what I said about green eggs and ham?
(Read from Dr. Seuss' book Green Eggs and Ham the lines about 'I would not like them here or there...'")

Dr. Seuss Hat: *"Those Dr. Seuss stories like in Green Eggs and Ham, Fox in Socks, and Hop on Pop make me want to talk in silly rhymes.*

I love how you talk Dr. Seuss Hat.

Dr. Seuss Hat: *"Yeah, that's the way I talk. Don't squawk, just walk. Watch my clock, seldom fly like a hawk, just talk and gawk.*

51

Dr. Seuss Hat, your funny, almost nonsensical lines, especially in *Green Eggs and Ham* remind me of tasty nutritious food much more appealing than Green Eggs and Ham.

Dr. Seuss Hat: *"Why so? What do you mean?*

I know of people who have little or no nutritious food. Ordinary eggs and ham would be quite delicious to them.

As Jesus' followers we get to share our food with the hungry – right here in America and throughout the world. So let's do what Jesus calls us to do – a food thing.

Dr. Seuss Hat: *Food dude, fresh food, no fake food, just preclude dog food, snack food, just food dude, helps your mood Jude!*

Thanks for the jingle, jangle Dr. Suess Hat.
Now, let's get serious. Let's write letters on behalf of Bread for the World. (explain)

Let's do a hunger walk where we collect funds for the hungry and starving. (add Third World hunger and development causes, local food pantry and other venues appropriate to the audience and setting)

Your marvelous hat, Dr. Seuss Hat, is tall and deep. Upside down it makes a perfect collection sack. Let's fill it with good things like food, money, prayer, and love for the poor and hungry. (make motions like you are putting items in the hat sack)

Let us pray,
Lord Jesus thank you for our food, shelter, pets, and toys. Give us a generous heart to share good gifts with others.
Amen.

A Parable in Mime
(A Chancel drama)

The following characters are in simple clown face makeup.

Characters: Father Clown
              Elder Son Clown
              Younger Son Clown – (spiffy at first, then and comes back a hobo clown)
              Angel Clown

Soft circus music in background

The Action:

Father Clown comes in on stage, busies himself with little tasks around the room.
Elder Son Clown comes in and talks to Father Clown. Elder Son Clown receives a list with detailed instructions for work around the room. He gets busy doing the tasks.

Younger Son Clown comes in receives a similar list and does a task or two but then begins to daydream. He displays a detached look while unenthusiastically continuing to work.
Father Clown gently touches him and reminds him of his tasks. The Younger Son Clown straightens a chair or two and then dreams on.

Younger Son Clown excitedly turns to Father Clown and indicates that he wants "stuff."
(money, property, and the like) Father Clown hesitates but eventually gives him many small boxes in a basket symbolizing "stuff."

Younger Son Clown goes skipping off and whistling a merry tune.

Father Clown and Elder Son continue to work and then sit down (freeze).

Back stage is a lot of commotion with loud music, laughter, and then a long silence.
After some time groans, moans, and crying is heard off stage.

Again there is silence. Background circus music is suspended.

Father Clown looks off into the distance. He climbs up a ladder in order to see further. He wrings his hands. He is obvious greatly sorrowed and distressed.

Suddenly the Young Son Clown reappears dressed as a Hobo Clown. He is black, dirty,and his basket is empty. He shuffles toward his father.

(Happy circus music begins again)

Father Clown runs and embraces Younger Hobo Son Clown. The Father quickly gives his son a new coat, new sandals, and a new hat, and gives instructions to servants who are off stage.

The two – Father Clown and Younger Son Clown skip down the aisle, arm in arm, while the Elder Son Clown moves to center stage, sits on a low stool and pouts.

The end (Happy circus music in background).

New Life In Abba's Arms
(A Message)

Luke 15:20-24 "So he set off and went to his father. But while he was still far off, his father saw him and was filled with compassion; he ran and put his arms around him and kissed him. Then the son said to him, 'Father, I have sinned against heaven and before you; I am no longer worthy to be called your son.' But the father said to his slaves, 'Quickly, bring out the robe – the best one – and put it on him; put a ring on his finger and sandals on his feet. And get the fatted calf and kill it and let us eat and celebrate; for this son of mine was dead and is alive again; he was lost and is found.' and they began to celebrate."

The son collapsed into his father's arms. The father shouted, "a robe, a ring, sandals, and a fatted calf!" The father called for a celebration, a party - for his son was dead and is now alive, was lost and now is found!

You know the feeling when something as minor as your set of keys is lost and suddenly found. Relief and joy sweeps over you.

Skip was a Lutheran Brotherhood agent in Mankato, Minnesota and a member of my church. His lovely wife Grace, the mother of his children, got ill and died. Skip was devastated. He grieved and grew lonely. Then after an appropriate period of time, Skip met Brenda and fell in love. They married and took a trip to the islands of the Dutch West Indies in the Caribbean Sea. One day I, their pastor, received a card stamped St. Martin, Guadeloupe, which simply said, "Arley, Yippee! Yippee! Yippee! Skip and Brenda."

This is what the father felt as he saw his younger son coming down the road – Yippee! Yippee! Yippee!

The father did not even give his son a chance to apologize. He pre-empted his son's begging by spontaneous forgiveness. He puts aside the son's pleas as completely irrelevant in the light of the joy at his return. Joyfully the father could not wait to give him new life, life in abundance. Nothing was good enough. The very best must be given – a robe, a ring, sandals, and a fatted calf.

The son returned tattered and barefoot.
Barefoot has always been a sign of poverty and slavery. Shoes are for the wealthy.
Shoes protect against stones and snakes. As the old African-American spiritual sings it:
"All of God's chillun got shoes. When I get to heab'n, I'm going to put on my shoes; I'm gonna walk all ovah God's heab'n."(in the public domain)

So the father dressed his son with the signs and symbols of freedom. He said in effect, "now wear this robe of honor, put on this ring of inheritance and wear the footwear of freedom and prestige.

Henri Nouwen pointed out that it was like an investiture by which God's favor was applied.
The full meaning of this investiture is previewed in the fourth vision of the prophet Zechariah in 3:1-10:
"God showed me the high priest Joshua standing before the angel of the Lord...Now Joshua was dressed in filthy clothes as he stood before the angel. 'Take off his filthy clothes.' And to him he said, 'See I have taken your guilt away from you, and I will clothe you with festal apparel.' And I

said, 'Let them put a clean turban on his head.' So they put a clean turban on his head and clothed him with the apparel: and the angel of the Lord was standing by....'If you walk in my ways and keep my requirements, then you shall rule my house, you shall have charge of my courts, and I will give you the right of access among those standing here. Now listen, Joshua, high priest...I shall remove the guilt of this land in a single day. On that day, says the Lord of Hosts, you shall invite each other to come under your vine and your fig tree.'"

The joy of this reunion and reconciliation is a continuing New Testament theme.
Jesus assumed that some of our richest joys are born not of laughter but of pain.
Pain is often present when we involve ourselves in the life of others. Our sadness
morphs into gladness when a loved one – long ill – gets well; or someone long absent comes home.

Jesus believed that the music of heaven is made out of the tears of the reconciled.

Jesus' parable of the waiting father climaxed three parables in Luke 15. In all of them about lost things, each transcended grief and danced in ecstatic joy. When the shepherd found his sheep, he rejoiced in the restoration. When the woman found her coin she exclaimed, "Yippee, yippee, rejoice with me!"

When the son came home, there was music, made in part of tears and in part of laughter.
Jesus knew that the joy of reunion makes the angels sing.

Jesus often pictured the kingdom as a roaring party – a joyful banquet – the centerpiece.
This invitation to a meal is an invitation to intimacy with God. This we happily celebrate in the Last Supper, "From now on, I tell you, I shall never again drink wine until that day I drink the new wine with you in the kingdom of my Father."

At the close of the New Testament, God's ultimate victory is described as a splendid wedding feast: "The reign of the Lord our God almighty has begun; let us be glad and joyful, and let us give glory to God, because this the time for the marriage of the Lamb...blessed are those who are invited to the wedding feast of the Lamb...."

Beethoven's "Ode to Joy" in his masterpiece, the Ninth Symphony, was composed under the most depressing circumstances. Beethoven composed the Ninth at the age of 54.
He was totally deaf and his health was declining. Beethoven was distressed by a Europe divided and laid waste by the French Revolution and the wars of Napoleon.

Beethoven took the words of the poem "To Joy" by Friedrich Schiller and wove them into the symphony. At its first performance, he could not hear the thunderous applause.

"Man is for joy and joy is for man. I think joy is not joy at all unless it is in man's possession" wrote Francis de Sales, "the human heart is so dependent upon joy, without joy, it cannot find rest. Joy is true only in so far as it is possessed by the heart of man."
(Francis de Sales was born in 1567 and served as a bishop in Geneva)

The spirit of the party is felt when hearing or singing a negro spiritual such as this one from the eighteenth or nineteenth century:

> My Lord, what a morning
> My Lord what a morning
> Oh, my Lord what a morning
> When the stars began to fall
>
> Oh you will hear all Christians shout
> 'Cause there's new day come about
> Looking to the Lord's right hand
> When the stars begin to fall.

Abba, is what Jesus called his father - and Abba stands with open arms.
It is a hug of joyful love and compassion.

Once Lincoln was asked how he was going to treat the rebellious Southerners when they had finally been defeated and had returned to the Union. The interviewer expected that Lincoln would seek revenge and destructive reprisals. But Lincoln answered, "I will treat them as if they had never been away." (Lincoln quotes)

So it is with Abba, our God, for you and me, because of Christ's atoning life, death and resurrection. We rest, we live, in Abba's arms, warmly loved and totally forgiven.

> Joyful, joyful we adore thee
> God of glory, Lord of Love
> Singing birds and flowing fountains
> Call us to rejoice in thee.
>   – Henry J. van Dyke (in the public domain)

Amen.

Week Six

"YOU'RE INVITED TOO, SON"

TALKING HATS
(Children's Mission Minute)

Props: Hats, Caps, and various Lids
Setting: Imagining a hat that talks – and oh, the story it tells

Mission Minute Six

Hello Boys and Girls,

Today I am wearing a very special lid—it's a New Year's Hat!
And along with my New Year's Hat comes all the hoopla that goes with it.
(blow noise maker, shake rattle, toot penny whistle)

What fun we have on New Year's Eve. We eat, we dance, we sing, we hug, and we kiss. It's party time – Happy New Year!

And like all the other talking hats in my collection this New Year's Hat talks too.
(a smiley face may be imprinted on the face of the hat)
Say hello, New Year's Hat to the boys and girls here today.

(take hat off and hold as puppet)

New Year's Hat: *Hi boys and girls. Yes, I am a talking hat. I love it when kids, and moms and dads too, wear me in happy, party times.*

Why so?

New Year's Hat: *"Well, a new year is about something new. New opportunities, new plans, new resolutions. A new year is a time to start over and to forget your past mistakes. It is a time to look ahead. Party time!*

Party time? New Year's Eve, birthdays, baptismal anniversaries, wedding anniversaries-- all kinds of times to celebrate and have a party. Then there's that party in the Bible. Remember?

New Year's Hat: *"Oh yes, yes – that parable Jesus told about the lost son. Well, the son in that faraway country finally woke up and came home to his Dad. And his Dad was so excited and happy he put on a party! That party was happier than any New Year's Eve you could ever, ever attend. They had a barbeque, and they found a ring and new clothes for the kid. Dad said, 'this my son was dead and is alive, he was lost and is found'."*

I agree Hat, that is an excellent reason for a party. That's really good news.
Feels really good to find something or someone that has been lost and then is found.
In our baptism we all have been found. Jesus found you and me. Now through the Holy Spirit, boys and girls like you get to tell your friends and neighbors about this good news of Jesus and what Jesus has done for them.

New Year's Hat: *You mean like spread the joy?*

You bet. Spread the joy buddies. Tell it. Sing it. Dance it. Have a party!

Let us pray:
Dear Jesus, thank you for finding us when we are lost. Lead us home when we stray.
Show us your love and forgiveness every day. Keep us safe. Keep us found.
Never let us go from your loving arms.
Amen.

2 Boys At Doc's
(A Chancel drama)

Setting: Medical doctor's examining room
Characters: Nurse Nelson
                 Dr. Bone Brake
                 Brother One
                 Brother Two

Nurse Nelson ushers two brothers in for their exam. He/She gives each a sheet to wear.

As Doctor Bone Brake enters the room Nurse Nelson begins to speak.

Nurse Nelson: Doctor Bone Brake, I have two brothers who have come for their physical. Boys be seated. You over here and you over there.

Doc: Hello fellows. It's good to see you. How are you?

Brother One: I'm fine. Don't really need this examination but Dad said we'd better get checked just to make sure we are all right.

Doc: I'm glad you're here. Sometimes something shows up and we need to address it. (Starts to examine brother one)

Nurse Nelson: And how are you? (to brother two) Are you having any symptoms?

Brother Two: Well, I didn't think so but then it began to happen and I knew I had to do something about it.

Nurse Nelson: Oh – what are your symptoms?

Brother Two: (whispers in her ear)

Nurse Nelson: Oh really. You'd better tell the doctor all about it after he finishes examining your brother.

Brother Two: I sure will. And how are you Nurse Nelson?

Nurse Nelson: (flustered) Oh, uh, I'm fine. You know I'm usually the one who does the asking here in this clinic, but it does feel good to be asked about me once in a while.

Doc: Yeah, I agree. I'm always asking "how are you" and when someone asks me "how are you?" I am surprised and pleased. It shows interest in a person beyond just clinic talk.

Brother One: (in a crabby tone) I don't care for chit chat in a professional setting.
Let's get to the point Doctor Bone Brake. What are you finding out about my condition?

Doc: (sits down and looks seriously at Brother One) Well my diagnosis is that you do have some problems.

Brother One: You must be kidding Doctor. I'm in perfect shape. I don't believe you.

Doc: No, just wait. I'll share my findings. First, we must wait for the cranial scan, the heart check, and the blood tests to return.

Brother One: Well okay. I'll wait. But I know it'll be negative. You just see!

Doc: (to Brother Two) And how are you?

Brother Two: Lot's of symptoms. Can you help me?

Doc: Sure, I think so. (examines Brother Two)

Brother Two: What are you finding, Doctor?

Doc: Well, my son, you have the symptoms of *lust lapses.*

Brother Two: Doesn't surprise me. I've been far away from home and.....

Doc: You also have *foolishness fever.*

Brother Two: No surprise there!

Doc: You also have *squandering* shingles, *big spender* bursitis, and humongous *careless* cellulitis.

Brother Two: *Lust lapses, foolish fever, squandering shingles, big spender bursitis, and careless cellulitis.* I plead guilty. What do I do about these ailments?

Doc: Change your lifestyle. Medicate yourself with love. Diet and exercise and hug yourself and others often. You'll see a rapid change. Trust me.

Doc: (turns to Brother One) Tests are in. Hmmmm. Let's see.

Brother One: I'm fine Doctor. If there's a problem in the blood test - it's got to be a mix up.

Doc: No, I'm afraid not. Here's what I found. You are suffering from *resentment rash, a bitterness burn, anger allergy and worst of all envy eczema.*

Brother One: No way, Doc. *Resentment rash? Bitterness burn? Anger allergy? Envy Eczema?* Don't believe it. You made this up. Prove it.

Doc: Oh yes, son, my diagnosis is accurate. Here's my prescription:
Follow this protocol. Like your brother – a definite change in lifestyle namely a change in attitude, perspective, a kinder heart, a long suffering patience and......

Brother One: Baloney! Forget it Doc. I am just fine the way I am. Send me the bill. All this just a waste of time. (stomps out)

Brother Two: Sorry Doctor about my brother's behavior. Thanks for exam. I'll do my best to take your advice.

Nurse Nelson: Wow. What a difference.

Doc: You can say that again. Too bad about the older brother – maybe someday he'll be back.

The Elder Son – Found or Lost?
(A Message)

Luke 15:25-32 "Now the elder son was in the field; and when he came and approached the house, he heard music and dancing. He called one of the slaves and asked what was going on. He replied, 'Your brother has come, and your father has killed the fatted calf, because he has got him back safe and sound.' But then he became angry and refused to go in. His father came out and began to plead with him. But he answered his father, 'Listen! For all these years I have been working like a slave for you, and I have never disobeyed your command; yet you have never given me even a young goat so that I might celebrate with my friends. But when this son of yours came back, who has devoured your property with prostitutes; you killed the fatted calf for him! Then his father said to him, 'Son you are always with me, and all that is mine is yours. But we had to celebrate and rejoice, because this brother of yours was dead and has come to life; he was lost and has been found.'"

The father was the real hero of Jesus' parable. His love was a love the younger son never understood. He sat on the roof-top watching the road. He ran to meet him. He sobbed and shouted, "a robe, a ring, sandals, and a fatted calf." He proclaimed, "my son was dead and is alive, was lost and is found."

This is a perfect place to stop. Even the Pharisees were nodding their heads in agreement. But Jesus didn't stop there. He couldn't. He went on to describe another character in the story – the fellow who stayed home.

Obviously, the elder son did well, at least in comparison to his younger brother. He was at least respectable. He had faithfully stayed home. He had virtues we admire today.
He was thrifty, industrious, and dependable. Today he would be eligible for membership in the rotary club or could easily serve on the church council. He would be a great candidate for school board, even perhaps the state legislature.

However, what we do know about him, quickly becomes crystal clear. He was ungracious. His goodness was bogus. True, he stayed home. He did the chores. He kept the rules. He sowed no wild oats. He wasted no money nor scarred his soul with dissipation.

But he was a sourpuss. One would hesitate to go fishing with him. He was touchy, stingy, churlish, and thoroughly wrapped up in himself. He did the right things, all of them in the wrong spirit that repelled and pushed one away.

At my first parish in South Dakota I preached a series of sermons on Jesus' parable.
Afterward, Al, who farmed nearby the rural church said, "I can't readily identify with the younger son – cause I stayed home and did everything right and yet I see the distant country in me like the elder son."

Jesus' story of two sons perfectly illustrates two definite expressions of sin – the sins of passion in the younger and the sins of temperament in the elder.
The lad who left home was simply giving in to the blatant passions and flamboyant sins of the flesh – the same passions and sins infecting our culture today.
"He squandered his property in dissolute living."

The son who stayed home betrayed the subtler sins of character. These are harder to avoid and easier to hide. He was overcome with envy. He expressed bad temper. He was self-centered and acted out social callousness. "...he became angry and refused to go in..."

Has the church historically attached more guilt to the sins of passion than to the subtler sins of temperament? Have we been harder on profanity than prejudice? Have we been more severe on adultery than anger? Have we focused too heavily on law rather than on love?

Looking into our souls and then into a "culture gone wild" one wonders which does more damage – lust or resentment? No doubt both.

There is among us "saints and sinners" infected with too much judgment, condemnation, and prejudices.
Henri Nouwen said, "I know from my life, how diligently I have tried to be good, acceptable, likable, and a worthy example for others, but in doing so I became less free, less spontaneous, less playful and ….more as a 'heavy' person...often I catch myself complaining about little rejections, little impolitenesses, little negligences...I discover within me the feeling that I must be the most misunderstood, rejected, neglected, and despised person in the world."

The elder son was unable to enter into the joy of the moment. Music, dancing, and laughter brought out the worst in him. He resented his brother. He condemned his brother. He rejected his brother. Joy and resentment cannot exist together. When one is deaf to the song and blind to the dance, one is lost!

One of their songs at that celebration might well have been Psalm 100:

> *Make a joyful noise to the Lord, all the earth.*
> *Worship the Lord with gladness;*
> *come into his presence with singing.*
> *Know that the Lord is God.*
> *It is he that made us, and we are his;*
> *we are his people, and the sheep of his pasture.*
> *Enter his gates with thanksgiving,*
> *and his courts with praise.*
> *Give thanks to him, bless his name.*
> *For the Lord is good;*
> *his steadfast love endures forever,*
> *and his faithfulness to all generations.*

But the sin of temperament, prevented the elder son from entering the celebration.

Yet the Father's embrace was ready. The lights were on in the house. The music and dancing was contagious. You could see the elder son standing outside the circle of love, looking in but refusing to join in.

Unlike a fairy tale, Jesus' parable provides no happy ending. Instead, it leaves us face to face with the hardest move of all, and that is to completely trust God's all forgiving love.
How will you and I finish the parable? Will the elder son in me come home? Can I be found as

the younger son was found? How can I return if I am swimming in resentment, when I am green with envy, and jaded by jealously? How can the father find me when I am imprisoned in myself, dutifully living out my responsibilities slavishly? Truth of the matter is, you and I need to be found again and again. I cannot heal myself. I cannot be born from below. I can only be healed from above. I can only be filled with joy and gratitude from the work and power of the Holy Spirit.

Luther put it this way: "I believe that I cannot by my own reason or strength believe in Jesus Christ or come to him but the Holy Spirit calls, gathers and enlightens me...."

Here's the ending to this parable that I would like: The elder son realized he was a jerk. He realized in a flash of insight that he too had been in a distant country of his own making and he needed to change. He hung his work clothes in the shanty and put on the robe his father had given him long ago, went in, and joined the party."

Martin Luther once had a dream in which he was in heaven watching the hand of Christ write in a great book the sins of Luther's life – one by one. As the list grew longer and longer and more shameful and more shocking, Luther could not stand the agony of it any longer. He was just about to cry out when he saw drops of blood coming from a wound in the hand that wrote it. As the blood of Christ fell on that long list of Luther's sins, it blotted them out completely, every last one. He remembered, "The blood of Jesus Christ his Son cleanses from all sin."

Oscar Wilde once said that the miracle of God's love is that, "It is eternally given to that which is eternally undeserving."

Come join the party! It's all grace - nothing more, nothing less.

Amen.

Bibliography and Resources

All I Need to Know I Learned From Hank Williams – Ethics Lessons From Country Music by David Fillingim, Sojourners Magazine, March/April 2000.

Balloons Aloft: Flying South Dakota Skies, by Arley K. Fadness, published by Xulon Press, May, 2013.

Horns and Halos In Human Nature, by J. Wallace Hamilton, published by Revell, 1954.

In the House of the Lord: From Fear to Love, by Henri Nouwen, published by Darton and Longman and Todd, 1986.

New Revised Standard Version of the Bible, Copyright 1989, Division of Christian Education of the National Council of Churches in the United States of America. Used by permission. All rights reserved.

One Step Closer, Why U2 Matters To Those Seeking God by Christian Scharen, published by Brazos Press, Grand Rapids, Michigan, 2006.

Pastrix by Nadia Bolz-Weber, published by Jericho Books, Hachette Book Group, New York, NY, 2013.

Six Spiritual Needs in America Today by Arley K. Fadness, published by C.S.S. Publishing Company, Lima, Ohio, 1998.

The Adventures of Pinocchio by Carlo Collodi, published by February, 1883.

The Case For Christ by Lee Strobel, published by Zondervan, Grand Rapids, Michigan, 1998.

The Cross and the Prodigal: Luke 15 Through the Eyes of Middle Eastern Peasants, published by IVP Books, 2005.

The Return of the Prodigal Son: A Story of Homecoming by Henri Nouwen, published by Image Books/ Doubleday Publishing Group, 1994.

The Waiting Father, by Helmut Thielicke, published by Harper and Row, San Francisco, 1959.

What's So Amazing About Grace by Philip Yancey, published by Zondervan, 1997.

Suggested Songs to listen to for the "feel" of this parable:
> "O Danny Boy"
> "Calling My Children Home" Emmylou Harris
> "Come To The Cabaret"
> "I Still Haven't Found What I'm Looking For" Afro-American Spirituals
> "Just As I am"
> "Amazing Grace"
> "Joy To The World"

A Feast for eyes and soul
Recommendation: Jerry Evebryde's *Prodigal Son Collection* of 600 pieces of visual art based on the biblical parable from Luke 15. This collection is archived at Luther Seminary in St. Paul, Minnesota.